General Instructions

Before You Begin ...

Consider how you will finish and display your stitched piece before cutting the plastic canvas.

Note that the measurements and stitch counts given account for *the stitched design only.*

If you will mount your stitched piece in a frame, compare the opening in the frame with the size of the stitched design. Allow for additional rows of unstitched plastic canvas around the design so your stitched piece will fit snugly in the frame. You can conceal any "extra" plastic canvas around the edges with a pattern of decorative stitching, or cover it with a mat cut to size.

You may choose instead to simply Overcast the edges of the stitched plastic canvas and display it by hanging it from yarn or ribbon loops, or sawtooth hangers stitched to the reverse side.

Alternatively, you could "frame" the central design with a decorative stitched border of your choosing. Again, be sure to cut your plastic canvas so that you have room for the additional stitching. And remember that you will need additional yarn.

Stitching

As much as possible, work in horizontal rows, stitching from left to right (if you are right-handed; left-handed stitchers should work from right to left).

Begin in the upper left-hand corner, bringing up the needle at the *bottom* of each stitch and taking it down at the top of each stitch. (In subsequent rows, if you bring the needle up at the top of the stitch, you risk snagging and distorting the stitch just above it, which will share the same hole.)

Begin stitching from the top of the design and work in horizontal rows toward the bottom.

Deer

Design by Mike Clark

Size: 11 inches W x 14 inches H
(27.9cm x 35.6cm)
Skill Level: Beginner

Materials

❑ 1 artist-size sheet clear 7-count plastic canvas
❑ Uniek Needloft plastic canvas yarn as listed in color key
❑ #16 tapestry needle

Stitching Step by Step

1 Referring to General Instructions, page 1, cut plastic canvas to correct size, joining graphs for top and bottom portions before cutting as one piece.

2 Stitch plastic canvas according to graphs.

3 Finish and/or frame stitched design as desired.

COLOR KEY	
Yards	**Plastic Canvas Yarn**
1 (1m)	■ Black #00
15 (13.8m)	■ Burgundy #03
11 (10.1m)	■ Maple #13
7 (6.5m)	☐ Cinnamon #14
28 (25.7m)	☐ Sail blue #35
1 (1m)	☐ Gray #38
5 (4.6m)	☐ Eggshell #39
1 (1m)	☐ Beige #40
1 (1m)	☐ White #41
Color numbers given are for Uniek Needloft plastic canvas yarn.	

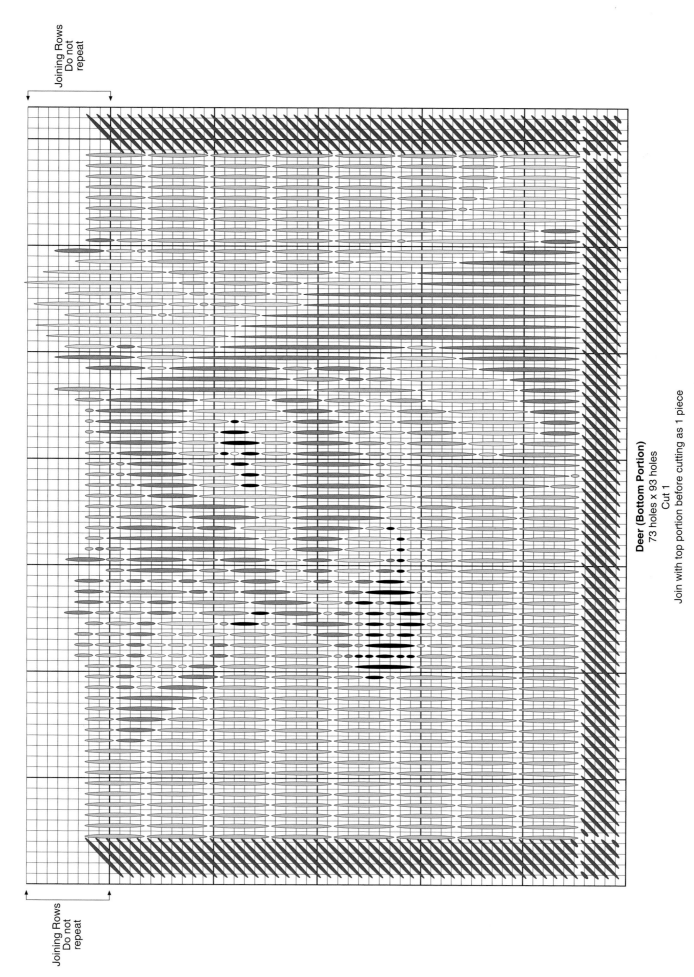

Joining Rows
Do not
repeat

Joining Rows
Do not
repeat

Deer (Bottom Portion)
73 holes x 93 holes
Cut 1
Join with top portion before cutting as 1 piece

The Needlecraft Shop • Berne, IN 46711 • DRGnetwork.com • **Nature's Wonders in Long Stitch** 3

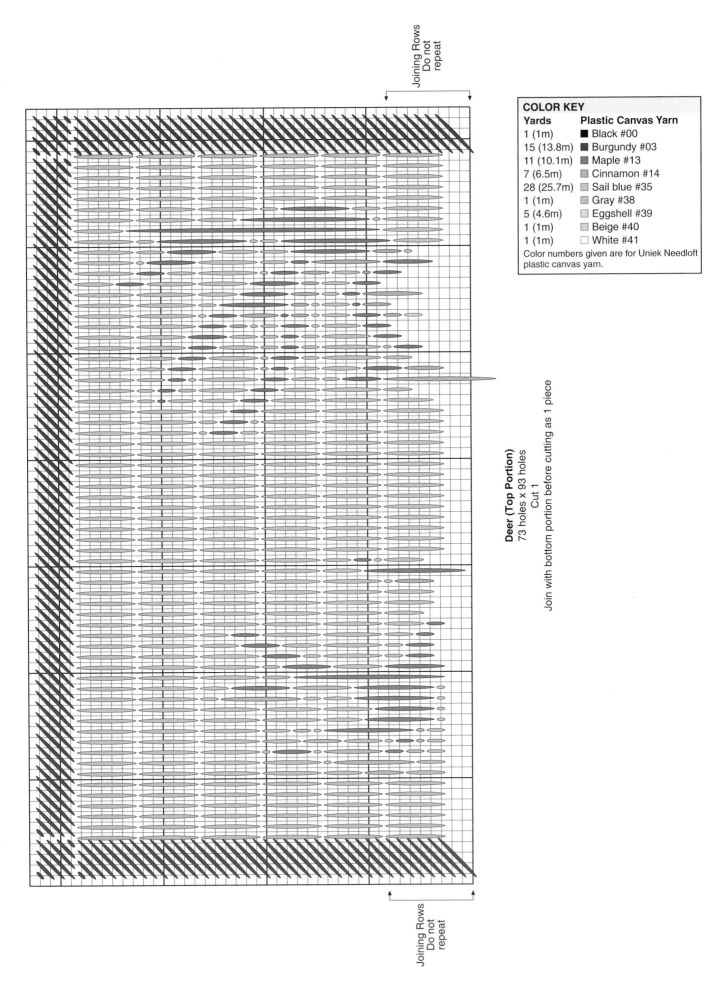

COLOR KEY

Yards	Plastic Canvas Yarn
1 (1m)	■ Black #00
15 (13.8m)	■ Burgundy #03
11 (10.1m)	■ Maple #13
7 (6.5m)	■ Cinnamon #14
28 (25.7m)	■ Sail blue #35
1 (1m)	■ Gray #38
5 (4.6m)	■ Eggshell #39
1 (1m)	■ Beige #40
1 (1m)	□ White #41

Color numbers given are for Uniek Needloft plastic canvas yarn.

Deer (Top Portion)
73 holes x 93 holes
Cut 1
Join with bottom portion before cutting as 1 piece

Joining Rows
Do not
repeat

Bighorn Sheep

Design by Mike Clark

Size: 11 inches W x 14 inches H
(27.9cm x 35.6cm)
Skill Level: Beginner

Materials

❑ 1 artist-size sheet clear 7-count plastic canvas
❑ Uniek Needloft plastic canvas yarn as listed in color key
❑ #16 tapestry needle

Stitching Step by Step

1 Referring to General Instructions, page 1, cut plastic canvas to correct size, joining graphs for top and bottom portions before cutting as one piece.

2 Stitch plastic canvas according to graphs.

3 Finish and/or frame stitched design as desired.

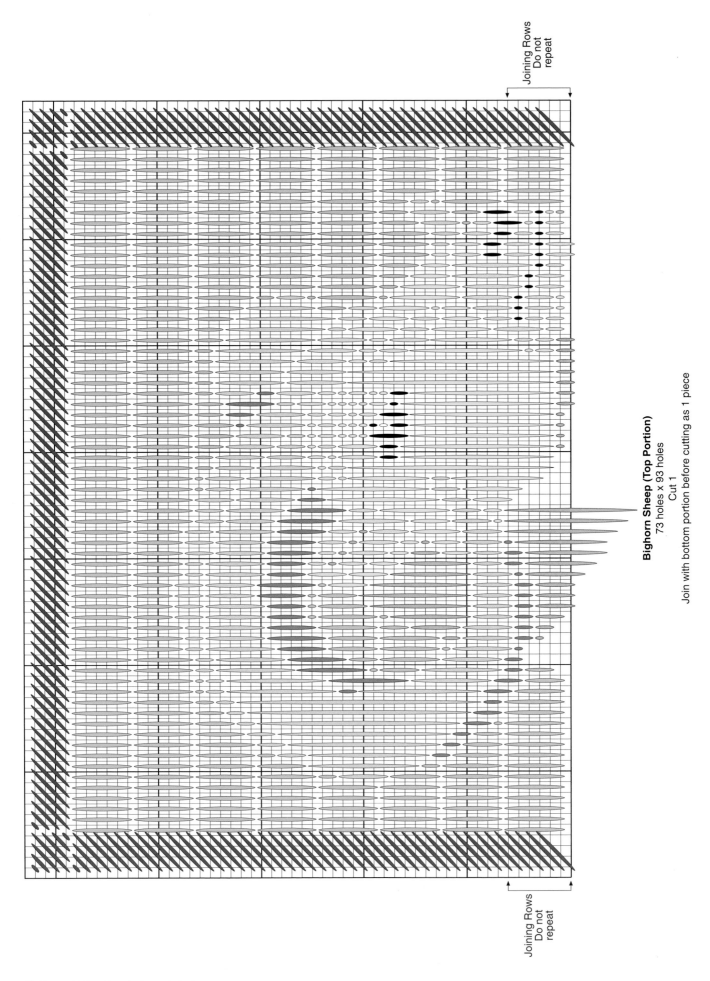

Bighorn Sheep (Top Portion)
73 holes x 93 holes
Cut 1
Join with bottom portion before cutting as 1 piece

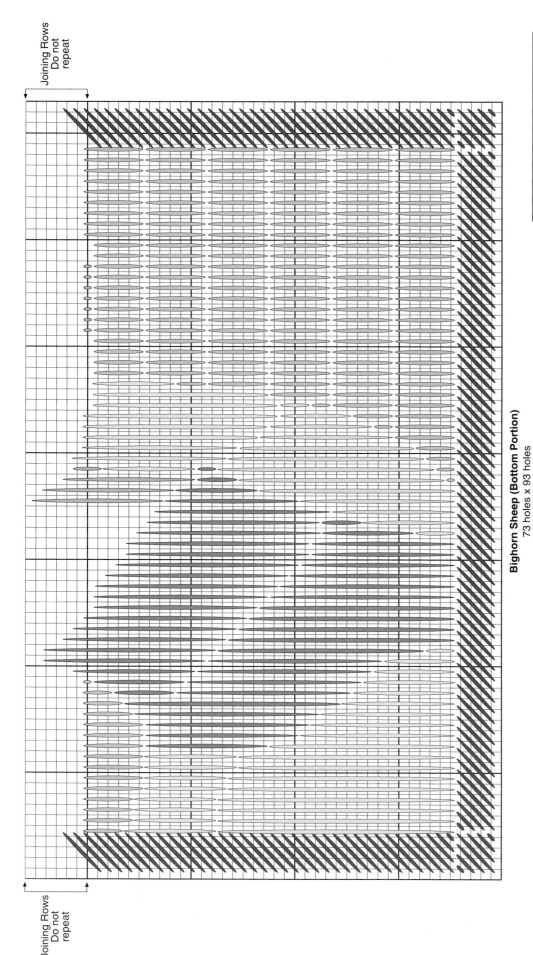

Bighorn Sheep (Bottom Portion)
73 holes x 93 holes
Cut 1
Join with top portion before cutting as 1 piece

Joining Rows
Do not repeat

Joining Rows
Do not repeat

Gristmill

Design by Mike Clark

Size: 9½ inches W x 7⅞ inches H
(24.1cm x 20cm)
Skill Level: Beginner

Materials

❑ 1 sheet clear 7-count plastic canvas
❑ Uniek Needloft plastic canvas yarn
  as listed in color key
❑ #16 tapestry needle

Stitching Step by Step

1 Referring to General Instructions, page 1, cut plastic canvas to correct size.

2 Stitch plastic canvas according to graph.

3 Finish and/or frame stitched design as desired.

COLOR KEY	
Yards	**Plastic Canvas Yarn**
1 (1m)	■ Black #00
1 (1m)	▨ Red #01
1 (1m)	■ Burgundy #03
2 (1.9m)	▨ Maple #13
3 (2.8m)	▨ Cinnamon #14
1 (1m)	▧ Sandstone #16
1 (1m)	▢ Gold #17
4 (3.7m)	▨ Holly #27
5 (4.6m)	■ Forest #29
4 (3.7m)	■ Royal #32
5 (4.6m)	▢ Baby blue #36
8 (7.4m)	▢ Eggshell #39
1 (1m)	▨ Dark royal #48
Color numbers given are for Uniek Needloft plastic canvas yarn.	

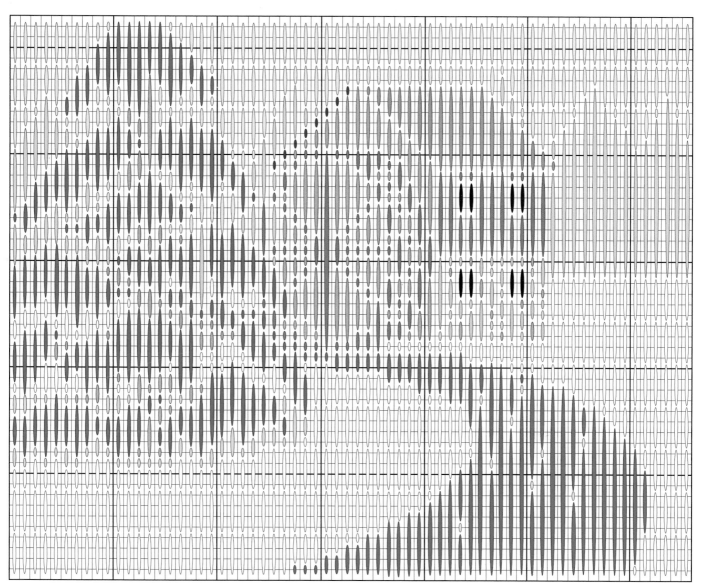

Gristmill
66 holes x 53 holes
Cut 1

Lighthouse

Design by Mike Clark

Size: 9½ inches W x 7⅞ inches H
(24.1cm x 20cm)
Skill Level: Beginner

Materials

❑ 1 sheet clear 7-count plastic canvas
❑ Uniek Needloft plastic canvas yarn
   as listed in color key
❑ #16 tapestry needle

Stitching Step by Step

1 Referring to General Instructions, page 1, cut plastic canvas to correct size.

2 Stitch plastic canvas according to graph.

3 Finish and/or frame stitched design as desired.

COLOR KEY	
Yards	**Plastic Canvas Yarn**
1 (1m)	■ Black #00
1 (1m)	Red #01
1 (1m)	■ Cinnamon #14
5 (4.6m)	Sandstone #16
4 (3.7m)	■ Holly #27
4 (3.7m)	■ Royal #32
13 (11.9m)	☐ Sail blue #35
1 (1m)	Gray #38
1 (1m)	Beige #40
5 (4.6m)	☐ White #41
Color numbers given are for Uniek Needloft plastic canvas yarn.	

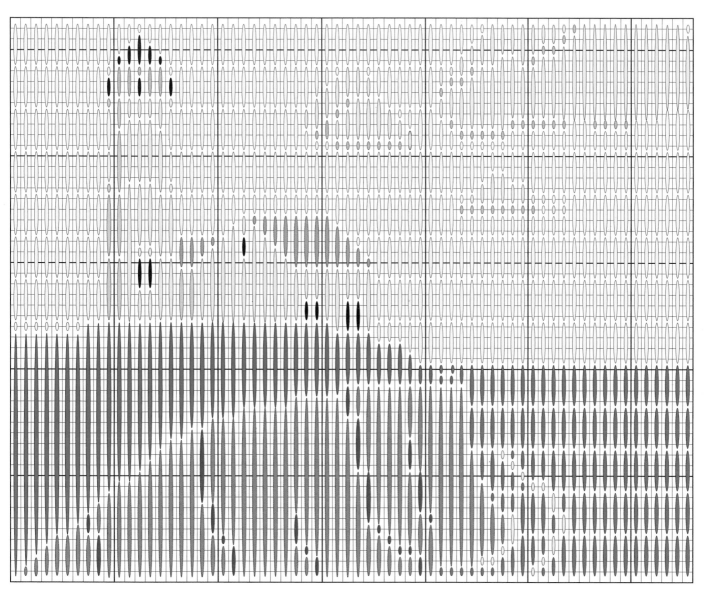

Lighthouse
66 holes x 53 holes
Cut 1

Mountain Lake

Design by Carole Rodgers

Size: 12⅜ inches W x 9½ inches H
(31.4cm x 24.1cm)

Skill Level: Beginner

Materials

❑ 1 sheet clear 7-count plastic canvas
❑ Uniek Needloft plastic canvas yarn as
listed in color key
❑ #16 tapestry needle

Stitching Step by Step

1 Referring to General Instructions, page 1, cut plastic canvas to correct size.

2 Stitch plastic canvas according to graph. Note that heads of canoeists are worked as Cross Stitches.

3 When background stitching is complete, work forest Straight Stitches at ends of tree branches that overlay background stitches.

4 Finish and/or frame stitched design as desired.

COLOR KEY	
Yards	**Plastic Canvas Yarn**
1 (1m)	■ Red #01
3 (2.8m)	☐ Cinnamon #14
4 (3.7m)	■ Sandstone #16
5 (4.6m)	☐ Fern #23
4 (3.7m)	■ Holly #27
7 (6.5m)	☐ Christmas green #28
9 (8.3m)	■ Forest #29
1 (1m)	☐ Royal #32
10 (9.2m)	☐ Baby blue #36
3 (2.8m)	☐ Silver #37
5 (4.6m)	■ Gray #38
5 (4.6m)	☐ Camel #43
3 (2.8m)	☐ Mermaid #53
13 (11.9m)	■ Bright blue #60
2 (1.9m)	■ Bright purple #64
	╱ Forest #29 Straight Stitch

Color numbers given are for Uniek Needloft plastic canvas yarn.

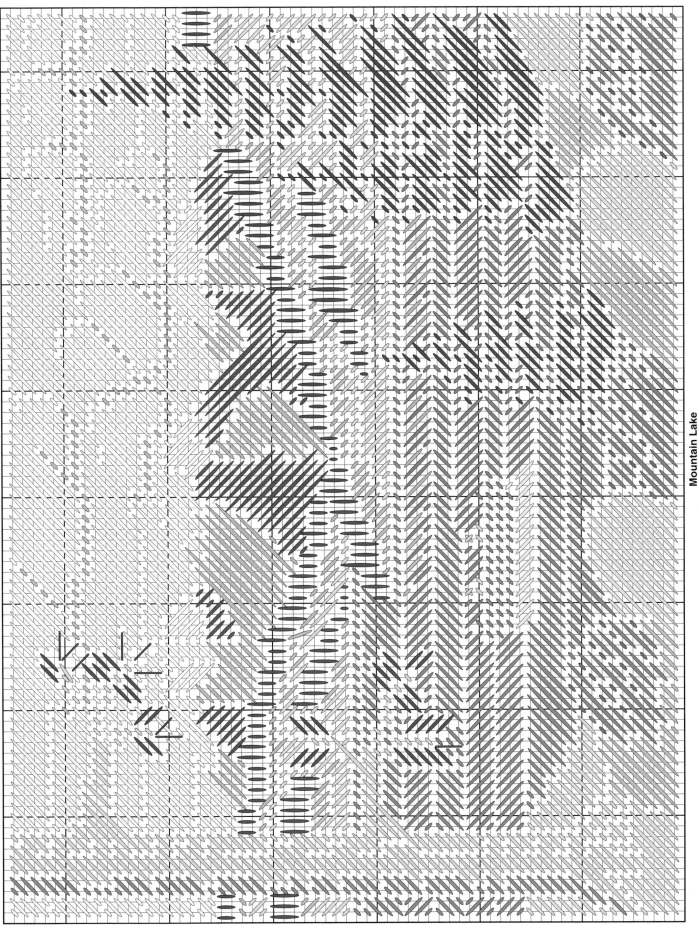

Mountain Lake
86 holes x 66 holes
Cut 1

Moose & Cabin

Design by Carole Rodgers

Size: 12⅜ inches W x 9½ inches H
(31.4cm x 24.1cm)
Skill Level: Beginner

Materials

❏ 1 sheet clear 7-count plastic canvas
❏ Uniek Needloft plastic canvas
yarn as listed in color key
❏ 6-strand embroidery floss as listed
in color key
❏ #16 tapestry needle

Stitching Step by Step

1 Referring to General Instructions, page 1, cut plastic canvas to correct size.

2 Stitch plastic canvas according to graph. Note that moose's eye is worked as a Cross Stitch.

3 *When background stitching is complete, work embroidery stitches:* Backstitch edges of trees using 6 strands gray embroidery floss. Straight Stitch cabin window using burgundy yarn. Work French Knots in waterfall with baby blue and white yarns according to graph, wrapping yarn once around needle.

4 Finish and/or frame stitched design as desired.

COLOR KEY	
Yards	**Plastic Canvas Yarn**
1 (1m)	■ Black #00
1 (1m)	■ Red #01
2 (1.9m)	■ Burgundy #03
5 (4.6m)	▦ Maple #13
6 (5.5m)	■ Cinnamon #14
5 (4.6m)	▧ Sandstone #16
8 (7.4m)	▧ Fern #23
6 (5.5m)	▨ Holly #27
7 (6.5m)	■ Christmas green #28
10 (9.2m)	■ Forest #29
2 (1.9m)	■ Royal #32
16 (14.7m)	☐ Baby blue #36
8 (7.4m)	▨ Silver #37
3 (2.8m)	▨ Gray #38
13 (11.9m)	☐ White #41
2 (1.9m)	▧ Camel #43
6 (5.5m)	▨ Mermaid #53
4 (3.7m)	☐ Light peach #56
9 (8.3m)	■ Bright blue #60
2 (1.9m)	■ Bright purple #64
	╱ Burgundy #03 Straight Stitch
	○ Baby blue #36 (1-wrap) French Knot
	○ White #41 (1-wrap) French Knot
8 (7.4m)	**6-Strand Embroidery Floss**
	╱ Gray Backstitch
Color numbers given are for Uniek Needloft plastic canvas yarn.	

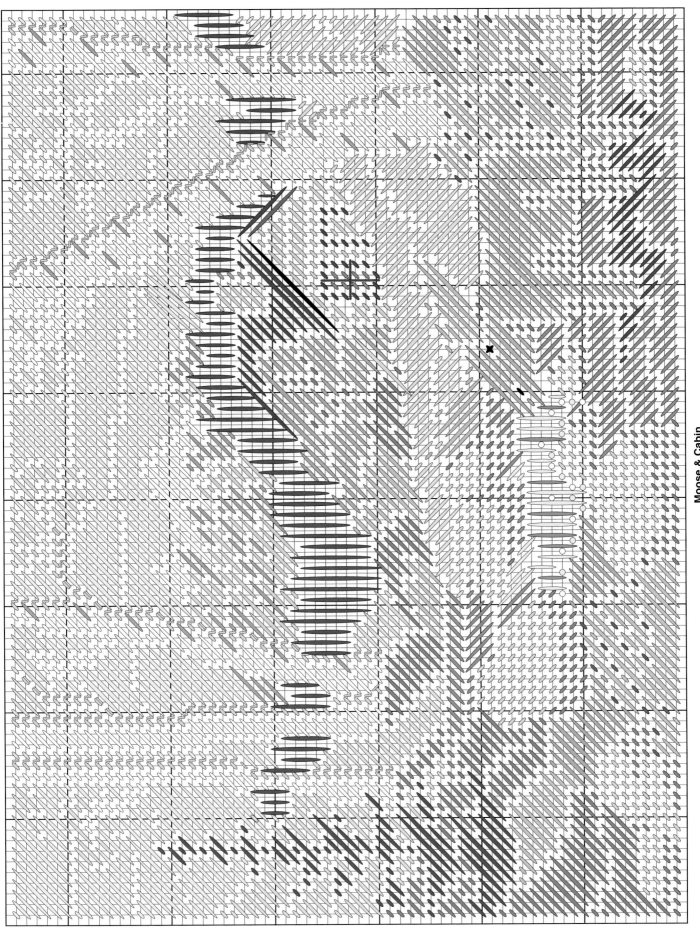

Moose & Cabin
86 holes x 66 holes
Cut 1

Southwest Eagle

Design by Mike Vickery

Size: 18¾ inches W x 11½ inches H
(47.6cm x 29.2cm)
Skill Level: Beginner

Materials

- ❏ 1 artist-size sheet clear 7-count plastic canvas
- ❏ Red Heart Classic Art. E267 medium weight yarn as listed in color key
- ❏ Red Heart Super Saver Art. E300 medium weight yarn as listed in color key
- ❏ #16 tapestry needle

Stitching Step by Step

1 Referring to General Instructions, page 1, cut plastic canvas to correct size, joining graphs for right, middle and left portions before cutting as one piece.

2 Stitch plastic canvas according to graphs.

3 Using 1 ply separated from a length of gray heather yarn, Backstitch and Straight Stitch around eagle according to graph.

4 Finish and/or frame stitched design as desired.

COLOR KEY	
Yards	**Medium Weight Yarn**
50 (45.8m)	☐ White #311
25 (22.9m)	■ Black #312
30 (27.5m)	☐ Gold #321
15 (13.8m)	■ Brown #328
20 (18.3m)	☐ Warm brown #336
7 (6.5m)	■ Mid brown #339
3 (2.8m)	☐ Light gray #341
1 (1m)	■ Vibrant orange #354
7 (6.5m)	☐ Lavender #358
10 (9.2m)	■ Paddy green #368
40 (36.6m)	■ Claret #378
25 (22.9m)	☐ Light blue #381
10 (9.2m)	■ Country blue #382
7 (6.5m)	☐ Soft navy #387
25 (22.9m)	☐ Gray heather #400
20 (18.3m)	☐ Light sage #631
10 (9.2m)	☐ Dusty teal #657
10 (9.2m)	☐ Emerald green #676
	╱ Gray heather #400 (1-ply) Backstitch and Straight Stitch
Color numbers given are for Red Heart Classic Art. E267 and Super Saver Art. E300 and E301 medium weight yarn.	

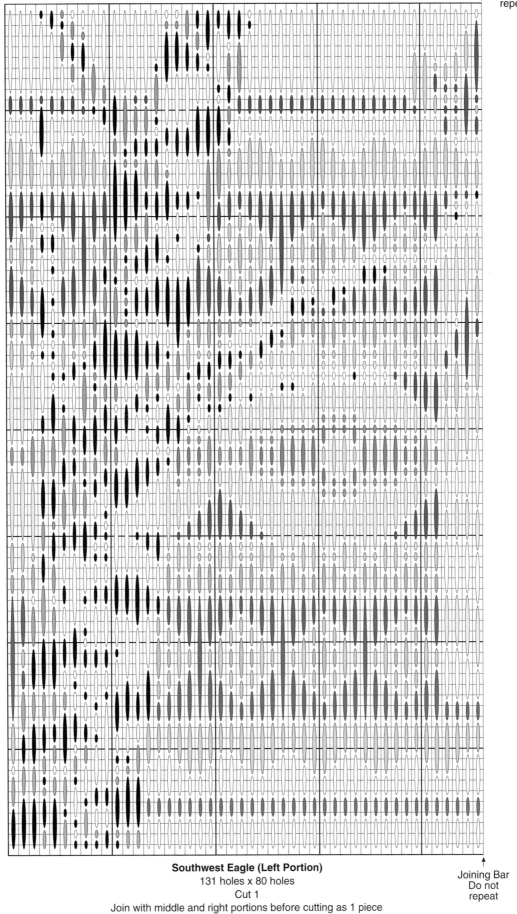

Southwest Eagle (Left Portion)
131 holes x 80 holes
Cut 1
Join with middle and right portions before cutting as 1 piece

Joining Bar
Do not
repeat

Joining Bar
Do not
repeat

Joining Bar
Do not
repeat

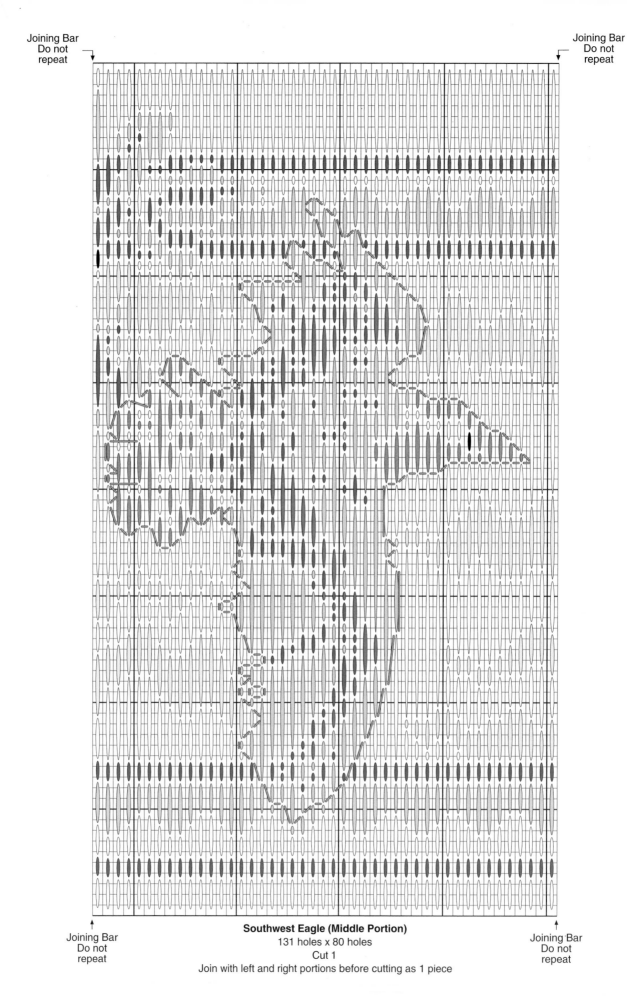

Southwest Eagle (Middle Portion)
131 holes x 80 holes
Cut 1
Join with left and right portions before cutting as 1 piece

Joining Bar
Do not
repeat

Joining Bar
Do not
repeat

Joining Bar
Do not
repeat

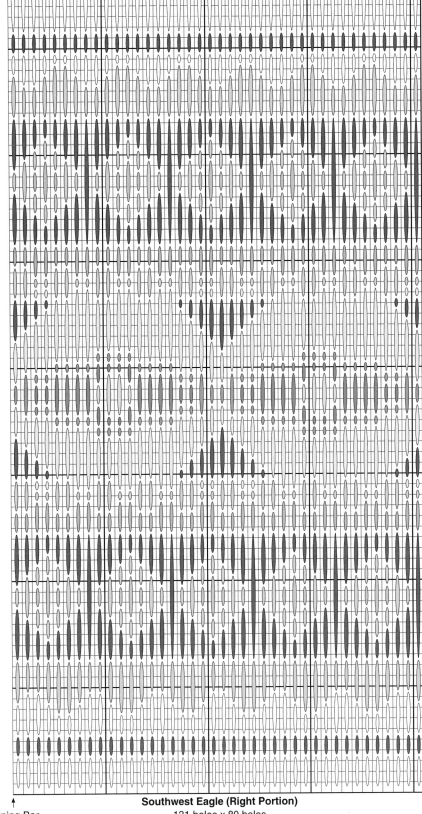

Joining Bar
Do not
repeat

Southwest Eagle (Right Portion)
131 holes x 80 holes
Cut 1
Join with left and middle portions before cutting as 1 piece

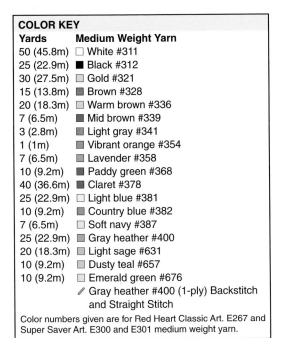

COLOR KEY

Yards	Medium Weight Yarn
50 (45.8m)	☐ White #311
25 (22.9m)	■ Black #312
30 (27.5m)	☐ Gold #321
15 (13.8m)	■ Brown #328
20 (18.3m)	☐ Warm brown #336
7 (6.5m)	■ Mid brown #339
3 (2.8m)	☐ Light gray #341
1 (1m)	■ Vibrant orange #354
7 (6.5m)	☐ Lavender #358
10 (9.2m)	■ Paddy green #368
40 (36.6m)	■ Claret #378
25 (22.9m)	☐ Light blue #381
10 (9.2m)	■ Country blue #382
7 (6.5m)	☐ Soft navy #387
25 (22.9m)	☐ Gray heather #400
20 (18.3m)	☐ Light sage #631
10 (9.2m)	☐ Dusty teal #657
10 (9.2m)	☐ Emerald green #676
	✎ Gray heather #400 (1-ply) Backstitch and Straight Stitch

Color numbers given are for Red Heart Classic Art. E267 and Super Saver Art. E300 and E301 medium weight yarn.

Young Hunter

Design by Mike Vickery

Size: 11½ inches W x 20 inches H
(29.2cm x 50.8cm)
Skill Level: Beginner

Materials

- ❏ 1 artist-size sheet clear 7-count plastic canvas
- ❏ Red Heart Classic Art. E267 medium weight yarn as listed in color key
- ❏ Red Heart Super Saver Art. E300 and E301 medium weight yarns as listed in color key
- ❏ #16 tapestry needle

Stitching Step by Step

1 Referring to General Instructions, page 1, cut plastic canvas to correct size, joining graphs for top, middle and bottom portions before cutting as one piece.

2 Stitch plastic canvas according to graphs.

3 Finish and/or frame stitched design as desired.

COLOR KEY	
Yards	**Medium Weight Yarn**
30 (27.5m)	☐ White #311
27 (24.7m)	■ Black #312
4 (3.7m)	▧ Aran #313
4 (3.7m)	▧ Cornmeal #320
7 (6.5m)	▨ Gold #321
10 (9.2m)	■ Brown #328
14 (12.9m)	▧ Warm brown #336
21 (19.3m)	▨ Mid brown #339
7 (6.5m)	☐ Vibrant orange #354
14 (12.9m)	■ Paddy green #368
10 (9.2m)	▧ Rose pink #372
7 (6.5m)	▨ Country rose #374
13 (11.9m)	■ Burgundy #376
7 (6.5m)	☐ Claret #378
9 (8.3m)	☐ Light blue #381
10 (9.2m)	▨ Country blue #382
9 (8.3m)	■ Soft navy #387
12 (11m)	■ Gray heather #400
10 (9.2m)	▨ Nickel #401
6 (5.5m)	☐ Light sage #631
12 (11m)	▨ Dusty teal #657
3 (2.8m)	☐ Emerald green #676
Color numbers given are for Red Heart Classic Art. E267 and Super Saver Art. E300 and E301 medium weight yarn.	

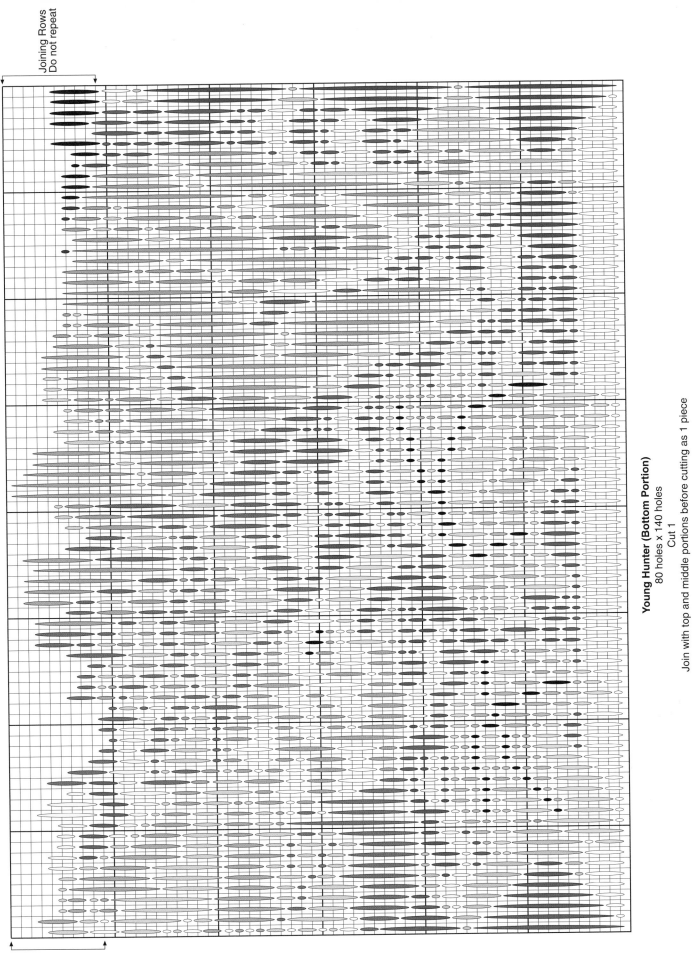

Young Hunter (Bottom Portion)
80 holes x 140 holes
Cut 1
Join with top and middle portions before cutting as 1 piece

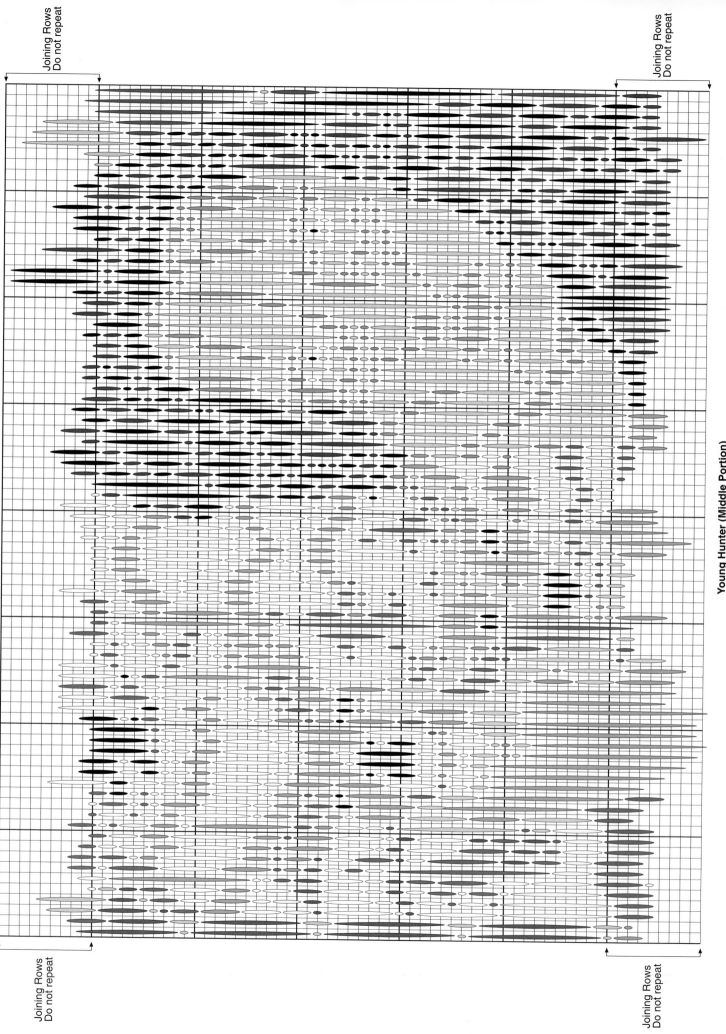

Young Hunter (Middle Portion)
80 holes x 140 holes
Cut 1

COLOR KEY

Yards	Medium Weight Yarn
30 (27.5m)	☐ White #311
27 (24.7m)	■ Black #312
4 (3.7m)	▨ Aran #313
4 (3.7m)	☐ Cornmeal #320
7 (6.5m)	▨ Gold #321
10 (9.2m)	■ Brown #328
14 (12.9m)	☐ Warm brown #336
21 (19.3m)	▨ Mid brown #339
7 (6.5m)	☐ Vibrant orange #354
14 (12.9m)	■ Paddy green #368
10 (9.2m)	☐ Rose pink #372
7 (6.5m)	▨ Country rose #374
13 (11.9m)	■ Burgundy #376
7 (6.5m)	☐ Claret #378
9 (8.3m)	☐ Light blue #381
10 (9.2m)	▨ Country blue #382
9 (8.3m)	■ Soft navy #387
12 (11m)	■ Gray heather #400
10 (9.2m)	▨ Nickel #401
6 (5.5m)	▨ Light sage #631
12 (11m)	▨ Dusty teal #657
3 (2.8m)	☐ Emerald green #676

Color numbers given are for Red Heart Classic Art. E267 and Super Saver Art. E300 and E301 medium weight yarn.

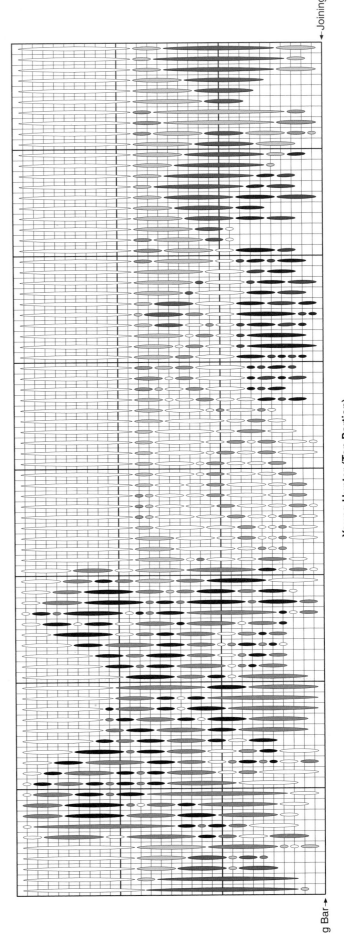

Young Hunter (Top Portion)
80 holes x 140 holes
Cut 1
Join with bottom and middle portions before cutting as 1 piece

The full line of The Needlecraft Shop
products is carried by Annie's Attic catalog.
TOLL-FREE ORDER LINE
or to request a free catalog
(800) 582-6643
Customer Service
(800) 449-0440
Visit AnniesAttic.com

We have made every effort to ensure the accuracy
and completeness of these instructions. We cannot,
however, be responsible for human error, typographical
mistakes or variations in individual work.

ISBN: 978-1-57367-309-9

Printed in USA

1 2 3 4 5 6 7 8 9

Shopping for Supplies

For supplies, first shop your local craft
and needlework stores. Some supplies
may be found in fabric, hardware and
discount stores. If you are unable to find
the supplies you need, please call Annie's
Attic at (800) 282-6643 to request a free
catalog that sells plastic canvas supplies.

Getting Started

Before You Cut

Buy one brand of canvas for each entire project as brands can differ slightly in the distance between bars. Count holes carefully from the graph before you cut, using the bolder lines that show each 10 holes. These 10-mesh lines begin in the lower left corner of each graph to make counting easier. Mark canvas before cutting; then remove all marks completely before stitching. If the piece is cut in a rectangular or square shape and is either not worked, or worked with only one color and one type of stitch, the graph is not included in the pattern. Instead, the cutting and stitching instructions are given in the general instructions or with the individual project instructions.

Covering the Canvas

Bring needle up from back of work, leaving a short length of yarn on back of canvas; work over short length to secure. To end a thread, weave needle and thread through the wrong side of your last few stitches; clip. Follow the numbers on the small graphs beside each stitch illustration; bring your needle up from the back of the work on odd numbers and down through the front of the work on even numbers. Work embroidery stitches last, after the canvas has been completely covered by the needlepoint stitches.

Basic Stitches

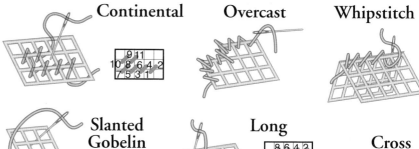

Embroidery Stitches

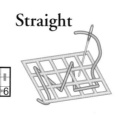

METRIC KEY:
millimeters = (mm)
centimeters = (cm)
meters = (m)
grams = (g)